How to Get Laid Off

Tina Stoufer

To everyone out there looking for a job.

TABLE OF CONTENTS

PROLOGUE

As I begin to write this book, I don't know if it has a happy ending or not. Right now I am four months into an almost eight-month severance package, and actively looking for a new job. The year is 2012, still well within the slow economic recovery period from the crash of 2008. My phone has not been ringing off the hook, but I feel like I am on the right track. I am doing everything in my power to get my career going in the direction I want it to go. It seems impossible that I will not find a job for years and end up on skid row. So what is the worry?

This book is not about how to underperform at work so that you are put on the "cut list." This book is about how to get laid off right. That is to say, in the inevitable eventuality that we will all be laid off at some point in our lives, there is a right way to do it so that you prepare, maximize your time, and actually wind up making changes that move your career forward.

This book is not written by a human resource specialist, attorney, career coach, or unemployment counselor. All of the content is the original thoughts of people who have actually been laid off. These are our real-life experiences and advice based on what happened to us. My hope is that it will provide a fresh look at layoffs and real-life strategies on how to bounce back.

As I looked for real-life stories beyond my own to add to this book, I did not have to look far—almost everyone I've ever worked with has been laid off at one point in their career. The most surprising thing I learned when interviewing my peers was how inspirational their stories were. Most of these people took the bull by the horns and used the opportunity to alter their career paths for the better. Even though there was significant fear involved, they got creative and used the time off to get additional training or experience, or to realign their career path. They all landed on their feet, and you can too.

CHAPTER 1

A Word About Layoffs

Layoff, downsizing, RIF, restructuring—these are words that most every worker knows, but doesn't like to think about very often. The term layoff used to mean a temporary suspension of work, but today, a layoff generally means you're gone. Permanently. Layoffs have been around for a long time. Where I grew up in Northeast Ohio, the auto industry has been laying people off and giving out early retirement packages for decades.

Still, it seemed like it was confined to certain industries and certain types of workers. If we have learned anything in recent years, it is that layoffs can happen in most any industry and any type of company. Some layoffs garner big headlines, and some are never heard of outside the company walls. But people lose their jobs, even if they work hard, and even if they have good performance reviews.

In 2009, a movie came out called *Up in the Air*, starring George Clooney. It was a movie about layoffs and a firm who executed them for other companies. The movie used some real people who had actually been laid off. Perhaps because I had worked in the technology sector for so long, I was surprised at how shocked and indignant the responses were of the laid-off people. It was like it was made thirty years ago. Were people really so surprised that they had been laid off—in this day and age?

It occurred to me that there was an opportunity to level the playing field in terms of knowledge and experience with layoffs. I have witnessed over a dozen layoffs—in all different shapes and sizes—in the companies where I have worked. I have seen people go through various stages of anger, stress, and grief, especially when they didn't see it coming. I don't want people to be shocked, unprepared, or anguished about being laid off. If I can provide some helpful advice to enable people to be accepting, prepared, and able to move forward with a plan, I will have achieved my goal.

It seems like layoffs are here to stay. Lifetime employment at a company and being "safe" because you do a good job are concepts of the past. A layoff can happen to anyone, anywhere. The sooner we accept it, the sooner we can adapt. This requires us to change the way we conduct ourselves and manage our finances and spare time. There is no reason for someone not to be prepared for a layoff, unless they reject this view and are burying their head in the sand.

This in no way means that I excuse the executives who get paid huge salaries and fail to provide the leadership and innovation to keep their companies successful over the long term, which would lessen the need for layoffs. It does not mean that I am not disgusted by the fact that whether they succeed or fail, many of these executives exit their companies with massive, golden parachutes and stock-option packages that regular employees will never see. It's not right and it's not fair, but it is reality. Rather than being bitter about them, figure out how to make your own golden parachute—or at least, a very sturdy aluminum one.

Understanding the modern layoff and learning how to adapt to the changing labor market will allow you to protect yourself, your family, your savings, and most importantly, your sense of self-worth and peace of mind.

CHAPTER 2

KNOW THE SIGNS

Part of being prepared for a layoff is being able to recognize when conditions are favorable for one to occur. Keeping your head down and your nose to the grindstone as your company directs you to do is fine, but don't be so cut off from the big picture that you get blindsided if or when the bad news comes down.

Here are some questions to ask yourself, when evaluating if a layoff may be eminent:

- Has your company's performance been in decline for a while?
- Have some of your coworkers already been laid off?
- Has your budget been cut multiple times?
- Has there been a moratorium on hiring?
- Has the company stopped issuing a dividend?
- Do approvals for even the smallest things have to be attained from high-level officers of the company?
- Does your company reorganize frequently?
- Are you increasingly taking on the workloads of other people who have left?

- Are you increasingly being asked to "do more with less"?

- Have raises, 401(k) matching, and bonuses stalled or halted?

- Has your company recently announced that it is being acquired or is preparing to merge with another company?

These are just a few of the signs you should look for. Other more overt signs include the obvious "rumor mill." Pay attention to leaks—don't just blow them off. Sometimes people are paranoid, but sometimes there is a grain of truth in what they say.

Anna, attorney

"You know, I think when the economy started to crash there were definite signs. The way it kind of started in our firm (and I think the way it started in some other firms) is at one point everybody had at least one legal assistant. It was one legal assistant for one attorney. And what they started doing was making it two to one. That was sort of the first tip-off. And then there was a year where they decided not to give raises to anyone, and then a year when they decided not to give bonuses to anyone. And so you kind of see it coming, and then they started laying people off in different departments."

It's important not only to read company announcements and quarterly earnings statements, but also to look at outside analyses, ratings downgrades, and message boards. Companies go out of their way to paint a positive picture internally in order to keep morale and productivity up. You may be getting some of the facts, but not the whole story. Always balance out what the company tells you by looking at credible, outside sources of information.

Previous layoffs are the best sign of an impending layoff. Especially if a company is going through a large-scale transformation—one shake-up usually does not do the trick. If there's one, there will be more. Don't ever assume it's over. Don't assume they won't come back for more.

Ryan, city planner

"I was laid off two different times, by the same company. The first time I was laid off, I was not surprised. The company had already completed three RIFs and closed a satellite office. I had a premonition that I would be included in the next round. I saw the CEO and other officers in one of the conference rooms. The door was closed and white paper was taped over the sidelight window. I knew it was coming. I heard a voice in my head say, 'Clear out your desk and print out samples of your work; you'll need them for job interviews.'"

Megan, advertising executive

"I had laid off my entire team that day, not knowing that I was also going to be laid off because I was told I was 'safe.' So I was already an emotional wreck because I loved my team and I had to tell three of them that they no longer had jobs. I told HR, 'I want to do all the talking, because they don't know you.' When they pulled me into the office to tell me I was going too, I was in shock."

Some people have a hard time believing it will happen to them. Sometimes if a person has survived one layoff or multiple layoffs, they believe that they are one of "the chosen." That the reasons others got laid off and they didn't are because they are special, more well liked, and a better performer than those people.

Some of the reasons people survive a layoff are:

- They work for a popular manager or have an executive advocate who is popular or powerful in the current regime. This will protect them for a while—at least until that manager or executive leaves the company, gets laid off themselves, or falls out of favor with the current or new regime.

- They work in an area or department that is still popular and thriving—for now. The way organizations are set up under one executive may change as executives are shifted around or as new leaders are hired from outside. But if certain business lines don't perform due to changing economic conditions or competitive pressures, those executives could be gone quickly. The web hosting division can be the hottest thing in the company one year, only to get decimated the next.

- They have consistently received excellent performance reviews. Being a good performer is always the best defense. But even the best performance cannot trump being in the wrong place at the wrong time. That can mean being in the wrong department at the wrong time, or physically being in the wrong location at the wrong time. Consolidation of offices as a source of layoffs can happen to even the best of employees, especially if a company is not open to remote work situations. One theory about the labor pools right now is that there are a lot of qualified people looking for work in almost any locale. They don't need the hassle of someone who works in a different time zone and can't meet in person at a moment's notice. Keep your performance at a high level, but recognize that it may not be enough.

I have witnessed many layoffs, and in my experience, rarely is it the case when only the "problem children" are let go. Layoffs are a numbers game. Don't assume that you won't get laid off because you are smart. Steve Jobs once got let go from Apple. It can happen to anyone.

That brings me to the primary reason people do not believe they will get laid off. They believe they are invaluable to the organization. They believe they have specialized expertise that doesn't exist in any other part of the company, and therefore, they cannot be let go. They were told at one point that their work was the future of the company. But let me tell you something: unless you are the single holder of the genius behind all of the deepest inner workings within the business, you are expendable. I know that's hard to hear, but it's true. "Even me?" you ask. Yes, even you.

So now that we have removed all denial that it can happen to you, we can move on with the steps you can take to be as proactive as possible and even have a very rewarding experience in the event that a layoff occurs.

CHAPTER 3

THE BACK-UP PLAN

Just like making a will, it can be unpleasant to sit down and really think about what you would do if you were laid off tomorrow. But it must be done. The more you think it out and write it down, the better prepared you will be for this eventuality and the less devastating it will be.

First, you have to look at what you would get if you were laid off. What does your company's severance plan look like? How generous is it? How many paid weeks of benefits would you receive? If your company had previous layoffs, details on the severance package should be available in their intranet somewhere.

Second, what do your finances look like? I'm not going to recreate a Suze Orman book, so I'll just point out a few simple concepts. Here are some questions to ask yourself:

- Do you have at least six months of salary in your savings account?
- How much debt do you have?
- What are your monthly expenses and which ones could be cut if you were laid off?
- Do you have other sources of income that can help support you while you are unemployed?

- How much would you receive from unemployment? Does your state allow you to collect unemployment while you are receiving severance pay?

Covering these first two areas will allow you to see how long you can afford to be unemployed before it starts to hurt. If you have been living paycheck to paycheck, running up bills and debt, then it's time to take a hard look at your spending habits and change your ways. If you have a substantial savings, a generous severance package, and other income, getting laid off may not be dramatic at all.

Ryan, city planner

"My wife used my layoff to win sympathy from her supervisor. He gave her more hours, which helped soften the blow. But it wasn't enough to make up for my income. Besides applying for jobs, I used my "extended vacation" to cook meals at home rather than eating out. I also sold things on eBay. I even started participating in those online surveys that pay you a buck after you've done like twenty of them. At least I didn't have to donate any body fluids!"

Depending on your profession, it can take a long time to secure a new job these days. There are some people who have been out of work for not just months, but years. Knowing where you stand and making the appropriate adjustments to improve your financial security are critical to surviving in these trying times.

Here are some possible areas to cut back if you get laid off. Create your own list or add to this one:

- Cable bill—Premium channels and services are unnecessary.
- Gym memberships—Expensive club memberships, training, or classes can be temporarily cut back in times of austerity. You can always run, walk, or use exercise DVDs and your own home equipment.

- Eating out, including coffee—This seems obvious, but should be mentioned because it can really drive costs up.

- Expensive groceries—Check your food bill and see how you can economize and downsize.

- Travel—It's difficult to enjoy vacations when you are worried about money, so put leisure travel off for a while.

- New clothing and shoes

- Mobile phone service—Go with a simpler plan or use a prepaid phone for a while.

- Landline phone—Cut the cord.

- Charitable donations—Take a temporary break, you are the charity now.

Anna, attorney

"We stopped going out for dinner. I stopped shopping altogether. We looked at cable bills and we just generally took a look at all of our bills across the board and looked to see if there was anything we could do to try to reduce. It sounds silly but I started using a lot of coupons at the grocery store. Even though things are a lot less dire now, I still retain a lot of those habits that I developed when it was really, really lean. So it's actually had a positive impact on me."

Megan, advertising executive

"I was much more aware of how much I was spending and how I was using my credit card and stuff like that. I think I also cancelled a lot of credit cards. I don't keep a lot, but I cancelled the credit cards that I felt like I really did not need, whereas before, when I was employed, I didn't really care. I cut out frivolous spending in phases rather than all at once because if I

did it in one fast move I would be resentful and that would add pressure to the job search."

Amy, employment law attorney/HR compliance

"We sold our house at a reduced price. We had bought our house based on my salary, and when I got laid off we couldn't really afford to stay there on Seth's alone. We also knew that I wasn't sure what I wanted to do with myself. I didn't know how long I wanted to be off. I didn't think I ever wanted that type of job again—at least not for quite a while. The high pressure, a lot of hours, a lot of travel, and after having my daughter I wasn't really sure I wanted to go back to that for at least ten years.

We decided that we should get a house that we could live on with Seth's income alone and not worry about whether I went back to work at a particular time. So we made a huge adjustment by selling our house because the market clearly sucked at that time. It took us ten months, and it depleted a lot of our savings to pay the mortgage for those ten months. Then we sold it at cost, so it interfered with our financial plans for sure."

When you are laid off, there are some investments that are beneficial to make because they will help you in your job search. Spend your money on things that will help you to get a new job, like classes, training, and networking activities.

Shirley, senior business manager

"I took classes at the community college getting ready for my Project Management Professional certification. So I did this different contract work and tried to keep my skills relevant, always looking at different business news and industry news, websites

online, and trying to keep up to speed on new technology. That's where I was most focused."

Another thing you can do to better prepare yourself for a layoff is update your resume. If you haven't done this in a while, it may be beneficial to have a professional review it and even pay them to rewrite it. If you've looked at your resume a thousand times, you may have difficulty seeing the flaws within it. If you are going to get serious about a new job search, make sure your resume is working as hard as it can for you. Think of this as an investment that will help you get interviews for better jobs and get hired faster.

You can also perform a skills assessment. Are there any skills required in the marketplace that you don't have? Are you up to speed on the latest technology? The time to acquire these skills is not after you get laid off, but while you are still working. There are two benefits to this:

1) You may be able to take advantage of your company's tuition reimbursement or development training programs. You really should be taking advantage of this type of program every year. It's money left on the table if you don't.

2) New skills, degrees, or certifications can be added to your resume to improve your qualifications. In this job-scarce environment, we all need to focus on keeping up with the market at all times. This will help you stay current on the latest knowledge and training, and make you more hirable.

What if your passion lies someplace other than your current job? This might be the time to start putting together plans to change careers or start your own business. If you have not already begun this process, the time has come to put some thoughts on paper and get the ball rolling. Again, the best time to start this is while you are still employed. Here are some questions to answer:

- What do you really enjoy doing?
- Do you have the skills to go into this line of business, or do you need more training?
- Do you have the experience to become a consultant in your area of expertise?
- Do you know anyone else who is successful in the profession who can advise you?
- Is there an association or networking group you can join to learn more about the business?
- What are the steps to get started in this new venture?
- What are the start-up costs?
- How can you support yourself and your expenses with this business?

Megan, advertising executive

"When you are laid off it is a really good time to make some other changes in your life. I thought I might as well make all big decisions now and move to San Francisco, and it was the best decision of my life. I wish I had the guts or the motivation to have done it sooner."

Here are a few items related to starting your own business that warrant a little more detail and thought:

Do you have others who can help you with opening a new business?

Starting your own business is a lot of hard work. Remember that you are not an expert in all aspects of business, so trying to cover all the areas yourself—and doing it well—is nearly impossible. You will need a support structure in place, even if it means enlisting independent contractors to help you run this business. Make a list of what you do well, then put some thought into areas where you may need to recruit help. Note that in a challenging economy, you'll need a lot of perseverance and dedication to realize your dream.

Are you trained in Internet marketing?

These days, a knowledge of Internet marketing, search engine optimization, affiliate marketing, pay-per-click advertising, banner advertising, and social media are critical for all businesses. If the list you just read sounds like Greek to you, it's time to go back to school. Even if you won't actually be doing it, you need to have an understanding of it, because inevitably you will be making decisions about it. People of a certain age may be resistant to becoming well versed in the Internet, and even more averse to delving into social media. But it is critical that you become aware of how these technologies work and how they can work in your favor to gain new business.

MeetUp.com

MeetUp is a great tool for networking with other small business owners and getting the word out about your business. It's free to join groups in most cases, and involves going to inexpensive luncheons where networking activities allow you to meet other people. It's good to have some materials to hand out. At a minimum, you should have your business cards. But if you have something else, a promotional postcard for example, those can be useful to hand out too.

CHAPTER 4

COMBATING NEGATIVITY

This is the most important chapter in this book because it is about your attitude during this difficult period. It doesn't matter how far ahead you saw this coming; when the layoff finally comes, you may have an unexpected emotional response. A lot of these responses are unproductive and will only suck up your energy and hold you back from finding your next position. You have to fight the impulse to be negative at every turn, and instead channel your thoughts and actions toward positive outcomes.

Anna, attorney

"Initially I was really mad because the reason that they gave me for laying me off was that the business wasn't profitable. I had a feeling that that was a lie because they had increased my billing requirement to the point where there is no way my department couldn't have been making money. And now that I am working in my own office, I know that I was profitable there because I am profitable now and I think that the problem wasn't me. I think the problem was that their overhead was really high because they made some bad real estate investments and were having to try to make up for that."

Why Me?

Why was I chosen? Why not him? Why not her? What's wrong with my work? Why don't they like me? You can ask yourself all day long why you were selected for a layoff. It may be personal, it may not be. You will *never* know the real answer. So why worry about it? You have to accept it and move forward immediately. Wondering why just wastes time and energy. And it doesn't matter. Let go of your pride. There have been so many layoffs in the past several years that practically no one blinks an eye when you tell them you've been laid off. Tell your story as objectively as you can to those who ask, and leave regrets behind. Believe in yourself and your abilities, and accept that you got caught in a bad situation that was neither a fit for you nor your employer. Focus on yourself and what's next.

I also recommend cutting ties with those still working at the company, or at least taking a break from regularly communicating with them. Checking in constantly at the old job just keeps you stuck in the past. You don't need to hear the play-by-play of what's going on there, good or bad. It's not your life anymore. Look forward. Five years from now, many of the people and much of the company will have changed so much that it won't resemble the place where you used to work. There won't be anything there to miss. The company might not even have the same name.

In a way, being laid off could be a blessing in disguise. In a layoff environment, the people who stay are most likely have twice the amount of work for the same pay—and are expected to be grateful. If you were lucky enough to get a severance package, use the time to your best advantage. With or without a severance package, the point is not to dwell on "why me?" but instead "what's next?"

Rachel, executive assistant

"Other people who were laid off met at my house for BBQ on the weekends. All brought food and beer. We talked about it together. Emotions bounced back and forth between anger and relief. The company was a sinking ship. Looking back, they did me a favor."

Hating

Here is a sample list of people you may hate if you get laid off: your boss, upper management, the president of the United States, all the people in the company who didn't get laid off, everyone in America who has a job, and worst of all, yourself. Don't waste time with hate. There may be some people to feel sorry for, but hate is not worth the effort. Bad things happen to good people. We don't know all the reasons. We all have to deal.

Anna, attorney

"I feel like with what's been going on in the economy over the last couple of years that there is definitely not so much of a negative connotation to being laid off. I think people realize that it is more a function of money than it is the function of someone's performance. I mean I don't love my former employer, but there are people over there that I don't hold a grudge against. I think I am kind of mad at them because some of the stress that I go through they are directly responsible for. I was very well liked at that firm by everybody, but I think that ultimately business is business and it comes down to numbers and it doesn't matter who the person is."

Scared to Death

Now is the most important time to believe in yourself. If you focus on the fear of losing everything and becoming homeless, it will not serve you well. Don't let yourself be paralyzed by fear. You have to move forward. Now. To be clear, the prospect of being out of work and not being able to pay your bills is scary. It is scary, but you must not be scared by it. You must stay positive, no matter what. There's no other choice, really. That doesn't mean that you can get rid of all worry. But you have to find ways to keep yourself "up." Your energy level is important to do all the things you have to get done. You have to be able to push on, even when it gets frustrating or discouraging. Therefore, look for inexpensive, stress-reduction activities that you regularly can do to give yourself a shot in the arm.

Megan, advertising executive

"I didn't get upset because I think I realized getting upset will just delay my trying to figure out what I have to do next."

Spero, marketing manager

"You have to have faith but you also need to look at this as an opportunity to try something new and different in your life, as opposed to just trying to go and getting the same, old job somewhere else."

Anna, attorney

"I really think staying calm and trying to come up with some kind of plan is absolutely the best advice. It seems like it's very overwhelming and like it's the end of the world, but chances are it's not. And if you stay calm you will realize that more quickly than if you panic."

CHAPTER 5

MODERN JOB SEARCH

Depending on how well you've prepared prior to your layoff, you are either way ahead on this or you need to get on it right now. Job searching in a tough economic environment is time consuming, discouraging, and frustrating. You have to keep at it. Never let up until you get something nailed down. Right now, your full-time job is to find a new job. So approach this like any project you've managed in the past; set search objectives and maintain a disciplined schedule. If your typical workday used to be anywhere between eight to ten hours, schedule four to six hours per day for job-search activity—whether it's working on your resume and cover letters, having lunch with someone in your professional network, or taking online training to enhance your job skills.

Be open to new ideas, locations, and salary expectations. I say this because the more narrow you make your search, the more difficult it will be for you to land a new job. Explore what your limits truly are. Here are some questions to think about:

- Are you open to relocating? If so, what geographic areas are you open to?

- What are your salary expectations? How low can you go and still pay your bills?

- How long of a commute can you tolerate?

- Are you willing to take a demotion in order to work your way back up in a new company?

- Are you willing to change industries, job descriptions, or areas of focus?

- Are you willing to do contract, part-time, or hourly work?

- Can you afford to volunteer your time to get experience in a new area?

- How long can you go without full-time employment before it starts to take a toll on your finances?

Amy, employment law attorney/HR compliance

"I took a job teaching as an adjunct instructor at a couple of colleges, which kept me working part-time and gave me great experience to move into things like training. So I wasn't actually out of work for two years, I was keeping current. After a couple of months I decided to see if I could make a move into human resources after working as in-house counsel after more than ten years. I took the first job I was offered, which only took about eight weeks to get. And suddenly I was in human resources."

Rachel, executive assistant

"I lowered my expectations regarding salary and accepted a job as administrative assistant making ten thousand dollars less. But now, after three years, I've moved on to another company as an executive assistant again and make more than I did at the time of the layoff."

Consider these things before setting up your online job searches or meeting with recruiters or outplacement groups. Give yourself the best chance to get a new job as soon as possible. Of course, you don't want to get yourself into something that is going to be a hardship and that you will not like at all. This exercise is just about finding where your boundaries really are and how flexible you can be. This is different from setting up a job search to find your next promotion or to get a higher salary while you are still employed, where you may have the luxury of targeting your ideal job. You may still be able to do that, but in challenging times you need to open yourself up and think outside the box.

Ryan, city planner

"The first time I was laid off, I did not consider relocation. I overestimated the market in my area. I kept thinking the jobs were there, I just needed to keep digging. After several months, I came to the realization that people in my profession were clinging to their jobs for dear life. Employers were either laying off or implementing a hiring freeze. The second time, I was wiser—and more desperate. Our family had grown from two to four. The COBRA premiums were crushing. I was now in full-blown crisis mode. I needed a real job—and if we had to relocate, so be it."

***

I'm not going to try to recreate what an outplacement firm or job-search book will tell you. But I am going to give you some ideas to explore that you can add to your own plan.

Outplacement Agencies

If your company provides these services to you, utilize them to the greatest extent possible. Use any resource that your company gives you for free. Some of the things that you may get from the outplacement firm are: in-person meetings with a career consultant, free resume advice, and online courses. Soak up everything you can. At a minimum, it will give you ideas for how to move forward. Take every bit of advice on your resume that you can get. People who work at outplacement firms have seen tons of unemployed people and their resumes. It's important to listen to them and what they are saying. Remember, this is their job— to help people who are out of work.

Your Network

Everyone knows that networking, networking, networking is the best way to look for another job. The first step is to let people in your network know that you are unemployed. Get over your pride and tell them. Chances are they've been laid off a time or two in the past, or have at least witnessed all the layoffs going on over the past few years. No one is surprised or shocked at layoffs anymore. Saying you are laid off can even be an advantage, because people are sympathetic to it. People want to help—they really do. They may not have an idea about a new job for you right away, but it will be in the back of their mind when something comes across their desk.

Rachel, executive assistant

"After accepting a lower-paying job, because I needed to take something to get off unemployment, I began networking. I even networked with vendors I met and kept putting my resume out there because I didn't want to settle for the position at a lower-paying job."

Talk to others who have been laid off along with you and get their input on job searching, saving money, or how they are spending their time off. Anything that can spark new ideas for you to explore is good. This is a time to be open-minded and consider new things that you may not have done for a while, especially if you have been working for the same company or doing the same job in the same town for a long time.

Megan, advertising executive

"I started reaching out to all my friends I've worked with to tell them that I was looking for a job. Whether you get laid off voluntarily or involuntarily, you feel disconnected from people. And that can be very lonely and it could be very depressing. It was like all of a sudden you realize you are not interacting with people the way you did before. Before you were going to an office where there were twenty people that you talked to on a regular basis and now, unless you make the effort, you are not interacting with people and that could be very isolating."

The most important thing about networking is to get out there and meet with people. Hit as many targets as possible, and something is bound to happen. The more exposure you get, the easier this will be. Make a list of everyone who might be able to assist in your job search. Some suggestions are:

- Family members
- Friends
- Former coworkers
- Former bosses
- Former classmates
- Former vendors and partners
- Associations
- Local networking groups
- Local social groups
- Online networking and social media

LinkedIn

This online network is a good way to connect with past coworkers and bosses. You can see where everyone is working and potentially find out if they are hiring. You can see your connections' connections and ask for an introduction if you don't know them personally. It's also a good way to see who does what at the companies you want to work for. If you secure an interview with someone, you can view their professional history, which will help you to better prepare. You can see if you have any background in common or if you have any mutual connections.

Online Job Sites

There are a lot of online job-search sites out there. Some are paid, but many are not. You will want to see listings of everything that is in your potential job market, so I recommend signing up with several of them. Scour them every day. Apply to as many as possible. Put the time into filling out all those annoying online applications and customizing your cover letter. Cast a wide net to give yourself as many options as possible. Back when I started out in my career, you had to look in the Sunday classified ads, print out letters and resumes, and mail them to employers. Online usage has made this process a lot more efficient. Hopefully, someday soon, we will have a system that allows you to put your resume into a standardized databank that all companies can draw from. But today, you have to enter it into each individual company's application system.

To find job search engines, simply type "job search" into your browser to see the top search results. If you are looking for specific industries or functions, add those terms to your search. Save job agents on those sites so that you don't have to set the same parameters each time you visit. Create both general and specific searches. Sometimes the general agents can produce lists that are too large to scan efficiently, but they will yield a greater number of results. Many may not be relevant to you.

Specific job searches with multiple criteria will produce fewer results, but they will be of a higher quality. By creating both broad and narrow search agents, you will be able to see more general listings when jobs that match your specific criteria are scarce.

You can also look at the job banks on the websites of specific companies in your area or companies that interest you. That is the only way to know for sure that you are seeing everything a company has to offer.

Articles and Books

Take time not only to look at job listings, but also career advice. Take a stroll through the career section of your local library or bookstore to see if any career books catch your eye. There are a lot of them out there, and many of them offer good advice you can use (like this one). Educate yourself about job searching and learn some new tricks. If you don't want to buy a book, there are many articles online as well about finding a new job. You never know where the good ideas are going to come from, so explore as many resources as possible. It doesn't hurt to read some books or articles that are motivational, to keep your spirits up and positive thoughts flowing during this time. Morale is very important, even while you are keeping your nose to the grindstone.

Shirley, senior business manager

"You have to trust yourself and tell yourself that you have what it takes and it's the numbers game. You make so many contacts per day and that will add up per week, and eventually you are going to hit the right job. And not every job that you interview for is going to be right for you. You will think, 'Oh, I could have said this, I should have said that.' No, you did the best you could, and it just wasn't meant to be.

I always kept that faith in myself that I knew I was good at what I was doing. And just because I got laid off, I was not going to let someone take my confidence away. But it did waiver because after you get into the market for a year—and in some cases, some people were in the market for over two years—it's hard. Their confidence waivers, and I tell them you've got to just keep at it. Take classes, do different things online, and make yourself feel good about who you are even without these corporate jobs. But I would be lying if I didn't say I worried about that next job. Because we get accustomed to that corporate life and that regular paycheck, and when it's not there you sort of feel off-kilter. It is just human nature."

Social Media

This section is not so much about how to use social media to promote yourself, but how *not* to use social media. Before you post anything on Facebook or Twitter, consider if it is something that you would be comfortable with a prospective employer seeing. Some people forget how visible these tools are. Even if you think you have tight security on your content, remember that your connections might be connected to a prospective employer. Sometimes we accept a connection with someone to whom we are not close, which means we don't know much about them, where they work, or who they know. It's better to be safe than sorry in this area. It's not a place for a free flow of thoughts. It could come back to bite you. Beware of what photos you post, too. It's a free country, and you can do whatever you want, but you have to present a more professional image to get hired. This shows prospective employers that you are social-media savvy as well.

CHAPTER 6

INVESTING IN YOURSELF

If you are laid off, it may seem like the most prudent thing to do is batten down the hatches, cut all expenses, and squirrel away every penny you can. But recall some of the things we have heard about corporations, and even our country—you can't cut your way to growth. There are some expenses that may be worth incurring if it can help make you more marketable to employers.

A Professional Resume

If you have redone your resume a dozen times and have looked at it so much that your eyes have crossed, it might be time to let a professional resume writer have a crack at it. Having friends review your resume and give you advice is great, but professional writers can elevate your resume to a new level. They can incorporate terminology that potential employers will use when they search online for the ideal candidate. Not everyone believes that paying to have your resume done is a good investment. There are a number of do-it-yourself books out there that you can use. But your friends or family may not be able to tell you everything that is wrong with your current document. Generally with resume services, you can receive a thorough critique for free. Then they will provide you with pricing to have them redo it.

Megan, advertising executive

"I thought I needed to sharpen up my resume, so I hired somebody because I am really bad at criticizing my own resume. I can look at a friend's resume and say, 'Oh, you need to do this,' but when I look at my own resume, I can't do it."

Generally, you get what you pay for with these services. There are some that will simply give you a questionnaire to fill out—where you essentially write the copy yourself—and they will put it in resume format for you. There are also services where all you have to do is get on the phone with them and answer their questions; they then go off and write the document for you. If you are considering outsourcing your resume, select a solution that fits your needs and budget. Be as thorough in giving information to the writers as you can. It's better to give them too much to work with than too little.

Education

Consider going back to school. If you are lacking a degree, it might be time to take out a loan to go back and get it. It can be expensive, but may be needed in order to make you a more attractive candidate. You may lack skills because you were in the same job for a long time, and new jobs require a background you don't have. If so, you can mitigate your lack of experience by adding to your education. If nothing else, it will allow you to learn the lingo of these new skills areas, and be able to speak intelligently on these subjects in interviews. And as soon as you start classes, you can add the program to your resume as a degree or certification in progress.

There may be certifications or licenses that would be beneficial for you to have. Peruse the job search engines to note the requirements of the jobs you are interested in. Certificates are generally much less expensive and quicker to complete than degree programs, yet can still be a powerful statement about your training and expertise.

If you are seeking a license, you can use it to do other work as a self-employed person while you are conducting your search for a full-time job. Who knows—your hobby or backup career may lead to starting your own business. At a minimum, a license helps you to get contract work, get listed in directories, and be part of a professional community. There may be associations that you can become a part of and network within.

An education is the greatest investment you can make in yourself. There are a variety of options now for people to go back to school, so there is almost no excuse for not doing it. Online education is on the rise, and allows you to take courses at your own pace from top universities and community colleges. Take time to explore what is available in your local area or in your interest area online. You may be surprised at how affordable some of these programs can be.

Shirley, senior business manager

"When I was working as a contractor for Verizon, I was already in school preparing for my PMP, and I knew that was always my goal—to just keep my skills sharp and add new skills. I knew the PMP certification was a coveted certification that all companies were asking for if you wanted to be a project manager. They don't even want to talk to you if you don't have your PMP certification."

Work for Free

Huh? Work for free? It sounds crazy, but you'd be surprised how many people will invite you to do projects for them when you are willing to volunteer your time or services without pay or benefits. I'm not talking about large corporations obviously, but small businesses are usually glad to take consulting advice or other services that you offer. Think of it as an adult internship. Here are some things that are great about offering to work for free:

Work Continuity

If you are working, regardless of whether or not you are getting paid, you are continuing to work. This can help address that pesky work gap on your resume. Instead of working on your resume and doing job searches all the time, try doing some actual work as well. If you are consulting with small businesses and providing deliverables to them, you are still working—and that is something that you can put on your resume.

The Ultimate Flexibility

If you are working for free, you can work as many or as few hours as you wish. You aren't obligated to anything—it's something that you work on when you have time. If the business wants you to start providing real deliverables in a specified amount of time, or wants you to devote a certain number of hours per week to them, that's when it might turn into a paid situation. It did for me.

Resume Building

If you are training or taking courses in new skills, an unpaid, informal, adult internship can be a way to try out those skills and get some experience with them in a real-world setting. I volunteered my marketing services at a fitness studio where I taught yoga. I offered up free plans, presentations, and analyses. After they saw what I could do, they wanted more, and started to pay me for the work.

I also helped them with their marketing calendar. Small business owners can get overwhelmed in trying to make a lot of improvements at once, so if you have skills in planning and organization, that can be of great benefit to them. While corporations might not be willing to hire you if you have the education but not the experience in a certain area, small businesses are far less stringent. They are more willing to let you try, as long as what you are doing is something that you can't irreparably screw up for their business.

And once you've done it for them—BAM!—you have new experience to add to your resume.

Amy, employment law attorney/HR compliance

"For about two years, I stayed home with my child—who was sixteen months old when I got laid off—so I took it as an opportunity to stay at home until she was ready for preschool. I also took the opportunity to do what I always wanted to do— teach college. So I taught undergraduate and graduate students at three different schools, and then decided to actually change my career path."

Spero, marketing manager

"I had never been in better shape in my life. I joined the fanciest health club you could join. I got to work out during the day when it was convenient. I bought a new laptop; I tried a multilevel marketing business as an entrepreneur. A lot of my time was for building the entrepreneurial business, but also doing yoga every single day."

CHAPTER 7

INTERVIEWING

I have two words for you regarding interviewing—prepare and practice.

There are a zillion books and articles out there on interviewing, and I don't claim to be more of an expert than many of these authors. These are just a few tips I can offer from my experience, which may be different from what you have read about before.

This should be obvious, but preparation is key for interviewing. I do not recommend throwing caution to the wind and going into interviews unprepared. The better prepared you are, the smoother it will go. The following are some tips to help you prepare and practice for interviews.

Preparation

Research the position, the company, and the interviewer, if possible. Thanks to LinkedIn, you may be able to get some background and even a photo of the person who is interviewing you. You may even find that you have some things in common in your background. Any way to form a bond is beneficial. If the job description provides details about the specific product lines or brands you will be working on, familiarize yourself with those. It shows that you were interested enough to make the effort to become familiar with the company. With access to the Internet, there is no excuse for not knowing anything about the company or job you are interviewing for.

Rachel, executive assistant

"Use examples when asked questions. Don't just give yes/ no answers. Bring questions and research information about the company. At my current position, my boss later told me how impressed he was with questions related to the company and specific questions that showed I was eager to understand my role."

60 Seconds and You're Hired, by Robin Ryan, is a great little book I found, which I have used to prepare for many interviews. This book gives you ninety potential interview questions and suggestions for how to answer them. It also offers advice on negotiating techniques, and gives a number of interviewing pitfalls to avoid. I actually typed out my answers to a lot of the questions and printed them out. I keep them handy for all phone interviews and pretty much have them memorized now. I paid specific attention to questions that could touch on my weaknesses and constructed good answers to those questions. Employers know that you are going to have weak points; it's how you address them that can make the difference.

This book also gives you a list of questions you should ask employers. Some interviewers want to be asked lots of questions about themselves, the job, and the company. This is to try to gauge your interest and enthusiasm for the position. I've never been comfortable asking a lot of questions because it seems a little presumptuous to ask such detailed questions about a job that you don't yet have. Nonetheless, the reverse-questioning method is something that is expected, so you have to be prepared. You can generate questions by using what is suggested in the book, by examining what is in the job description, or by researching the company website. You can also ask the interviewer more about themselves and their background at the appropriate stage. These questions can work if it appears that you are trying to get a feel for the backgrounds of the people who work there and what the culture of the company is like.

Ryan, city planner

"Landing a job you really want is a lot like dating someone who is out of your league. You hope they don't figure out you're not as confident as you appear to be. You remain calm but engaged, patient but assertive. You try to anticipate their next move, and how you should respond. And your response is what matters the most. Applications, interviews, even during training...they will make judgments about you based on your response."

I was looking for a job during the year of a presidential election, and found it interesting to watch politicians answer questions and give speeches. If you think of yourself as a politician and that you are trying to get your message across and engender trust, it can help you to be more confident in interviews. Pick a politician whose style you find compelling, and study how they give answers and communicate their message. Some of them are pretty slick. You don't want to be as evasive as a politician in answering an interviewer's question, but you can take a cue from them as to how to construct an answer with confidence and speak for the appropriate length.

Practice

Go on as many interviews as you can to hone your skills. Don't waste your time on jobs that you aren't really interested in, but don't be overly selective, either. Get comfortable being in the hot seat, and interviewers will be more comfortable with you. Note which questions they asked that you were not prepared for, and work on writing up a creative answer in case it ever comes up again.

You are inevitably going to have to discuss the circumstances of your leaving your last job. Be open and positive, without giving too much detail. Employers at this point are fairly nonplussed about people who have been laid off; they just don't want to see any red flags. Stay objective and fairly positive on the company that laid you off, providing a brief explanation of your understanding of the circumstances that led up to your release. Don't trash the company or talk about how screwed up it was there—even if it was. Show that you have a positive attitude and focus on how industrious you have been with your time off. The more you practice giving this explanation, the easier it will get. It's usually just a brief conversation, and then you can move on with the interview.

Shirley, senior business manager

"I used to fret about some interviews I would go on. 'Oh, why didn't I get that?' When I look back, I am like—oh my God, I would have hated that job. The best advice is to don't always be so eager to jump at the first thing that someone may offer you just because you feel that it is just not moving fast enough. One quote that my mother used to always tell me is if it's for you, you are going to get it, and I am a true believer in that. If it's not meant for you, it just won't happen."

Don't forget the advantages that a laid-off candidate has. A laid-off candidate can be available to start immediately, without giving notice to their previous employer. A laid-off candidate has had time to rest and revitalize, and is eager to start their next job. And hopefully the laid-off candidate has used their time off wisely to get some additional training or education. It's a time to show off your resilience in the face of adversity, which can actually work in your favor against employed candidates who are disgruntled with their current employer or are just looking for a higher salary.

Create a Portfolio

Collect your work samples and reference letters, and place them into a portfolio that can be a visual aid in your interviews. I have also created some charts that show the functions of the project teams I managed and of the overall functions I had responsibility for. These are not only a great explanatory visual for interviewers to see, but can also help you explain your experience more smoothly. Try to read the interviewer to see if they are interested in seeing your portfolio. Sometimes they are more interested in talking to you than in looking at your book. But other times they are very interested and impressed that you have it. If you bring it with you and set it obviously on the table, they will become aware that you have something to show them. But don't turn it into a show-and-tell session where you go through a long monologue about your past projects. They may start to glaze over. Keep the interview interactive and check in with them about what they want to see.

CHAPTER 8

WAYS TO GET YOURSELF HIRED QUICKER

Sometimes the need to land a new job becomes urgent. Time runs out to find the ideal thing, and you just need to get employed so that you can start getting benefits and have some income rolling in. Here are some ways to hit the accelerator, if it gets to that point.

Accept a Lower Salary

When I say a "lower salary," I mean, how low can you go? Half of your last salary? How low can you go to cover at least your biggest bills? It will significantly widen your pool of jobs. It is a judgment call as to how low you need to go and when. But sometimes getting a lower-paying job sooner is better than waiting for a higher salary. I know of a couple of people who took lower-paying jobs for a year—even thinking of them as an internship—to get experience and close their employment gap, then moved onto higher-paying jobs. This interim step may be necessary to get back into the game.

Amy, employment law attorney/HR compliance

"I would say, take the time off before you start panicking about what your next job is going to be and really dive into it. It's a great opportunity to say, 'What do I really want to do with my life?' because I got stuck in 'I am always going to have to be an attorney' instead of saying, 'What would I really enjoy?' Train yourself to be in the frame of mind of what you actually deserve, and negotiate. Do not ever take the first offer—even if you are unemployed—because if you do it right, and you're respectful, they are not going to rescind the offer. They may try to get away with offering you a little bit less if you are not working, and assume you will take it. Don't leave money on the table, even if you are unemployed, because they are not going to rescind the offer."

Conduct an Exhaustive Job Search

The job search should be done every day, for a few hours per day. Exhaust all resources online and investigate everything. Make sure you are seeing everything that is available. Back in the day, we could just get out the Sunday newspaper and see all the jobs in the marketplace. Now they are dotted around the Internet on various websites. Again, go to the websites of individual companies to see their job listings. Don't assume that all available jobs are picked up on the search engines.

Be Willing to Relocate or Have a Long Commute

This can be very inconvenient or even painful, but it might be necessary to get back into the job market. Try not to think of these changes as permanent. Maybe you just need to move or tolerate a longer commute for a few years, and then you can get back to where you want to be or move closer to the office. There are, of course, family considerations that will impact your ability to expand your options in this way. Depending on how dire your situation is, you may have to ask loved ones to make some sacrifices. What's most important is your family's financial security. Some honest conversations may be necessary. In difficult times the decisions are hard, but the hope that conditions will improve and the motivation to persevere will get you through these rough periods.

CHAPTER 9

HOW NOT TO GET LAID OFF

It may seem counterintuitive to include a chapter like this in this book, because most of it is about accepting layoffs and not wasting a lot of time wondering or fretting about how or why these layoff decisions were made. There are many circumstances where you cannot possibly guess or influence how layoffs come about. I have seen a lot of dysfunctional behavior from people who attempt to behave in a way that they think protects them from getting laid off. It's often counterproductive because it takes the focus off of doing what is right for their customer or their company, and puts it on internal company politics and a weird game of corporate Darwinism. In most companies, no one is truly 100 percent safe from a layoff.

But, all that said, there are a few pieces of productive advice I can offer to help you minimize your odds of getting laid off—the key word being "minimize." In the end, all the strategies in the world will not help if there are larger decisions being made that you have no awareness of or input into. But a few tips can't hurt, right?

Become Recognized as a Top Employee

Your best defense is a strong offense. If you feel like others on your team are more favored by management, do what you can to compete more effectively and better position yourself to be number one in the group. Being the last one standing doesn't mean that they won't eventually cut the number-one person, but at least you'll buy some time. If you are in a situation where certain people are the boss's favorites and you know you'll never rank above them, try to find another position internally where you can shine. Track your accomplishments religiously, and have regular performance reviews to get a feel for where you stand.

Work at Headquarters

If you really want to keep your job and you work in a remote office, moving to where the headquarters is may be advantageous. People who are in remote offices, away from top management, can become "out of sight, out of mind" after a while. This is particularly true after there have been several organizational shifts, and you no longer know the people you work for very well. Headquarters is generally the safest place to be because management can have more of a bird's-eye view of the talent they have, and more efficiently redeploy resources when needed. It also saves on travel expenses. In addition, a lot of people of an older-management generation still have the habit of not trusting people to work remotely, and would rather see them sitting in their cubicle every day to know that work is going on. If they don't know you personally, it's easier to cut you.

Shut Up and Do It

In tough times, companies like people who can take on off-the-wall projects, administrative tasks, and extra work without complaint—regardless of how ridiculous the task seems. If you are overly critical, stubborn, or contrary about what is being asked of you, you could become more vulnerable. If you are very interested in staying with your company and not getting laid off, this is a time to demonstrate your flexibility and willingness to work within the current environment. As annoying as it may be, just going along with it will make the path smoother. If your job is vulnerable, it may not be a good time to question or complain about projects that seem ridiculous on the surface. Your boss may be fulfilling twice as many ridiculous tasks, and you aren't even aware of it. Layoffs are a time when people who are difficult to deal with can get whacked. But if you just can't hold back voicing your opinion, roll the dice and see what happens. Every company is different.

Do Important Work

Has there ever been a group at your company that you looked at and said, "I never see one thing that comes out of that group. What the heck do they do?" Can you guess what eventually happens to groups like that? It doesn't matter if they've been around forever or if they are some executive's pet project; layoffs catch up to everyone eventually. Are you in one of those groups? Or is what your group does of critical importance, highly recognized by executive management, and a function that is clearly linked to stated, top objectives? If the latter—good, stay there. But continue to check in. Priorities can change over time. If you feel momentum shifting away, you have to do something about it. Go to work in a different group, or insist on getting involved with important projects. Become instrumental in getting your team more high-value work. Don't just wait for the ax to fall. Being relevant and producing relevant work can help extend your tenure—but this requires being honest with yourself. If what you do is not considered relevant, accept it and take the steps to make a change.

EPILOGUE

As it turns out, my story did have a happy ending, so I felt credible enough to finish this book. Like so many other people I know, I landed a job right at the tail end of my severance package. I don't know why that is—it's like the forces in the universe know how much time you have and then present you something right when you need it. I actually had a couple of offers from which to choose.

All the work I did during my time off was directly responsible for my getting a new job. The new resume, the consulting, and the additional education were all extremely valuable. It's very difficult to go back to school when you are working full time. And if you already have your degrees, there may be little motivation to do so. However, degrees get old. There are new technologies and new subjects to learn that can be very helpful to have on your resume.

I cherish the time I had between jobs—spending my days as I wanted to spend them, if just for a little while. I gained a lot of clarity on what I wanted to work on next, and I channeled that into my job search. Even though there were periods of stress, I needed to take a big risk in order to make change happen.

I think the biggest mistake people can make in their careers, especially once they have been in the workforce for a long time, is to become complacent. If you don't plan for being out of work, or keep up with your education, or actively manage your career path, you become more and more vulnerable. While it's nice to feel comfortable and not look for a job or go back to school, you should always plan to do something periodically to enhance your resume. Be alert, get experience or knowledge in the things you want to do, and check in with yourself and your career along the way. It would be nice if the economy stabilized and grew so much that we didn't need to worry about cutbacks and layoffs. But in the case that it doesn't, being prepared and accepting will ensure that when the ship goes down, you have built your own life raft.